THE GHOST OF YOU

A COLLECTION OF POEMS BY
R J O'DONNELL

THE GHOST
OF YOU

R J O'DONNELL

Trigger Warnings:

THE GHOST OF YOU contains explicit language, descriptions of self-harm and references of suicide. If any of the content is distressing, please consider contacting the supports below.

Lifeline WA- 13 11 14

Beyond Blue- 1300 22 4636

To all those who broke my heart

look how strong it still beats

you could not break me

CONTENTS

DEAR READER,

When I set out to put together this collection of poems, I didn't hold back. This collection is a snapshot of my soul, in all its raw and ugly glory. It is my journey from adolescence to now and my healing process all in one.

Some poems I wrote when I was sixteen years old- barely old enough to understand what love actually was, or who I was. They were my shout into the void, the desperate attempts of a girl figuring out her place in the world. The majority I didn't write until I was much older- when I was going through some of the greatest challenges of my life. Poetry became my therapy, a way to process what I was thinking and feeling.

The reason I decided to publish something so deeply personal is simple. I hope this reaches someone who has felt (or is currently feeling) as desperate and alone as I was. I hope that these poems can give them a sliver of hope that someone else out there knows what they are going through- that they are not alone. Poetry was there for me when I needed it to carry me through the dark; I hope that mine can return the favour.

For some of you that know me, undoubtedly, you'll feature in this body of work. If you think a particular poem is about you, then you're probably right. You may not like how you are portrayed, and that is to be expected. Everyone is the hero of their own story; it doesn't mean you're the hero in mine. I won't apologise for that. At the end of the day, this is my story. I've told it the only way I know how- through my own perspective. Be that as it may, I hope you enjoy the journey.

I know I did.

R J O'DONNELL

PART I – SHATTERED

STAND-OFF

We both know it's over

a stand-off in time

guns loaded, fingers twitching

neither of us ready

to pull the trigger

If you shoot first, darling,

I promise to bleed

SHATTERED GLASS

You ask how we can fix it
as if there was anything we could do
to piece together the shattered glass
you threw to the floor

Sometimes it's better to walk away
than to spend countless nights
picking the shards from your fingertips

A feeble attempt to put it back together
is still just a feeble attempt
no matter how you phrase it

Why should we waste
anymore of each other's time?

TRAIN TRACKS

Communication was not

our strong suit, we agreed.

Well,

let me communicate this:

There is nothing you can say

or do to stop this.

We are on a train

barrelling down a hill

with no hope

and no breaks

destined to collide

with the rocks

at the bottom.

There will be no slowing this.

There will be no survivors.

The end is inevitable.

You made sure of that.

RHETORICAL

Why is it

all my problems started

after I met you?

YOU SET THE DEMONS FREE

You stole the air

 from my lungs

but not in a good way

Never has a person

made me so

wracked with anxiety

You said you'd help

that together we'd keep

the demons at bay

And now you're the one

who's unlatched the cage

and set them free

How can I trust someone

who changes their face so easily?

THAT'S NOT WHAT I MEANT

When I said I wanted a burning love

I meant I wanted passion

I didn't mean

that I wanted to get burned

Even the coolest flames

still scorch, apparently

SEARCH HISTORY

How do I stop being angry?

How do I learn to trust again?

How do I sleep alone in our bed?

How do I forget the last five years?

How do I stop missing him?

How do I move on?

EMPTY SPACE

It feels like I'm missing a limb

[There's an empty space where you once were]

and even though it was gangrenous and
rotting

[and even though I'm better off now you're
gone]

I still feel the ache of where it used to be

[I still feel the ache of where you touched me]

THE GHOST OF YOU LIVES HERE

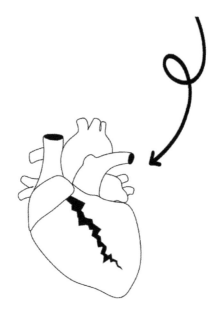

… Where did you go?

SLEEPING ALONE

Nighttime is when I miss you most

the moonlight softens the blow

of sleeping in an empty bed

If the light hits just right

the shadows fill the space beside me

it seems like you're really there

Until I reach out

my fingers aching, searching

grasping at nothing but air

GHOST

It's been a while since

we've talked, darling

each day we're apart

the further you fade

What do you look like?

the picture is all vignetted

I can't quite make it out

you're blurred around the edges

I struggle to recall the

taste of your lips

on mine

hungry in the dark

You're a ghost to me

forever haunting

always in my periphery

I can't let go

SHELL

I should have known

that when I poured myself

into your broken shell,

you'd leak me out;

Leaving you still broken,

and me empty.

HOPELESS ROMANTIC

I'll try and sleep
but it will be useless,
because I keep thinking
of how it ended between us

And even when I sliced myself open,
it didn't hurt half as much
as what you did to me

But I have a feeling we'll talk again soon,
because you said you were
a hopeless romantic,
and I've found out
I am one too

THE GHOST OF YOU STILL HAUNTS ME

I can still feel your presence

in the house

like a disgruntled spirit

The blank space where

your stuff once was

your shape pressed into the couch

The places you touched

the smell of you

still lingers there

Even though you're gone

I can't escape you

the ghost of you still haunts me

PLEASE STAY WITH ME

I've never known panic

like I did when you

were pulling away from me

I've dealt with anxiety;

I've had the air trapped

before it could reach my lungs

I've felt the knots

tying themselves in my stomach

and the impulse to run, run, run

Nothing compared to

the thought of you leaving

it was all I could do

not to scream;

please stay with me

ANXIETY

The darkness pulls me down

filling my lungs, stretching them,

no room for air

My lungs expand, search

never finding their fill

my head spins and I sway

unable to find solid ground

My chest aches for the times

I took air for granted,

holding my breath,

waiting for change

that never comes

Silly girl,

look how bad

you need it now

WAVES

Inky waves in the dark night

crash on the shore

white noise drowning out

violent, intrusive thoughts

The cold wind whips

biting into bare skin

better to feel numb from the cold

than numb from within

THE PRICE TO PAY

The beginning doesn't matter
as it all just ends the same
the numbing ache inside my chest
and the relieving vein

I wish I didn't need to
but I've so much to gain
a taste of life for the small price
of scarlet down the drain

I don't know how to feel
have I gone insane?
I'm not one for the blood
but I sure do like the pain

LOSING BATTLES, WINNING WARS

My wrist is a tally
I'm always keeping score
if I keep on losing battles
how am I to win the war?

My mind is a hurricane
intrusive thoughts are deafening
if my own brain is against me
how can I fight this thing?

My chest is a blackhole
the darkness swallows hope
if I cannot feel but emptiness
how am I to cope?

My face is a mask
it hides this all inside

what's the point of continuing

when my will to live has died?

My body is a graveyard,

where my aching limbs are stored,

I lost too many battles,

I couldn't win the war.

NOTHINGNESS

People say that I will hurt

that getting over you will take time

that I'm still raw and bruised

But time is inconsequential

I'm not still reeling

I do not ache for you

I feel nothing

I am nothing

Can you come back from nothingness?

THE PURGATORY OF DARKNESS

The darkness is an ocean, an abyss

it swallowed me

and I sank

On the way down

I threw about my aching limbs

and learnt to swim

I float now on the surface

not out,

not in

MALIGNANCY

The darkness sinks

its teeth into my bones,

a malignancy.

It wraps its tendrils around

my blood vessels,

infiltrating until

I cannot tell where I end

and it begins.

To kill it would be to

kill myself.

I will not give it the satisfaction

of winning.

I will not. I will not. I will not.

PUNCHLINE

Sometimes I think the Universe is

having a fucking joke

and I'm the punchline

Can I catch a break

or must she be cruel

to be kind

Only time will tell what'll go first;

her will,

or my mind

TAROT

My tarot cards said that you were

my soulmate

I think they were lying

Oh god, I hope they were lying

THE DARK

I used to be afraid

of the dark

until it sank its claws

into me

pouring black into my lungs

until I couldn't breathe

spinning my mind

blurring my eyes

until I couldn't see

twisting my spine

and shaping my soul

until it took the last of me

Now, I am the dark

and I am not afraid

But you should be

PART II – REBUILD

TIME

They say time heals

and helps you move on

but I'm starting to find

the more time I spend

away from you

the more I don't want to

HOW LONG IS THIS GOING TO TAKE?

I still dream about you...

(When will you get out of my head?)

A TWIST OF FATE

I never used to believe in fate

but how can I deny

what's been in front of me

this entire time

Less of a twist of fate

and more of a 180

how can the person

who fucked me, save me?

MANIFESTING

I'm over you.

I'm over you.

I'm over you.

If I keep telling myself that

eventually, it'll be true…

DONE

Some days it's hard

not to reach for you

you're a bad habit

I need to kick

I don't need you

though my body

tells me I do

it's just a symptom of loneliness

Stay away or

I'll lose my resolve

and call you right

back to square one

It's not fair

to circle back to

one another

it's best we're just done

CROCODILE TEARS

Crystal eyes, glimmering bright
brimming with remorse
do you feel bad for what you've done
or just that you got caught?

Crystal eyes, glimmering bright
shining with regret
"would you take it all back?"
as if I could forget

To be without me; your greatest fear
you're blowing up my phone
spare me your crocodile tears
you just don't want to be alone

SPITE IS A POWERFUL MOTIVATOR

I bathe myself in sunlight

to chase away the darkness you left

that threatens to claim me

I eat all things sweet

to wash away the bitterness

of your taste on my tongue

I wrap myself in soft blankets

to dull the sharpness

of the feelings you gave me

I refuse to be dark

and sharp and bitter

I will remake myself into something better

Not because of you

but to spite you, to show you

that I'm no quitter

NOTHING I CAN'T DO

There is one thing you forgot

when you left me

and that is

there is nothing I can't do

and that includes

leaving you too

IT'S TIME

It's time to move on

pick yourself up, my love

no one else is going to do it for you

It's time to move on

leave the past behind you

it has served its purpose

It's time to move on

you deserve better than what he gave

now go get it

I DESERVE MORE

The reality of it is

it doesn't matter what you say

it doesn't matter what I feel

I can't go back

I deserve more than that

I'VE OUTGROWN YOU

You're a winter sweater

I am in the summer

basking in the glow

I needed you once

not anymore

I'm better on my own

FINALLY

Finally,

I can see

I *am* enough

and all this time

the only one

I needed

was me

PART III – LONGING

WAITING

All I want is for

someone to look at me like

I put the stars in the sky

For someone to know

every part of my soul

and still want me as I am

I crave a love so full

our hearts spill over

unable to contain it all

I hold onto the hope

that I'll find it one day

I know it will be worth the wait

CITY

He was a city,

mighty and tall and proud,

with lots of lovely little things

occupying his many streets.

I wished to trace my fingers over

his alleyways,

to feel the beat of the traffic

pouring through his tunnels.

I longed to taste his bitter air,

tainted by cigarette smoke and whisky

breathe it into me

like a brisk wind whipping through

crowded streets.

Let me wipe away the April rain

dripping from the eaves

so his street lamps may shine

bright once again on me.

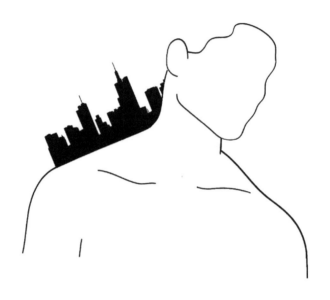

TOO GOOD

You're too good to feel alone

my darling,

so I'll whisper my 1 am secrets to you,

just to make you feel at home

You're too good to be empty

my darling,

so I'll pour my messy 2 am thoughts

 into you,

just to make you feel whole

You're too good to hate yourself

my darling,

so I'll spill my 3 am heart

all over the floor,

in the hope you'll love yourself

a little more

MAYBE

Maybe you're not mine

maybe you're not meant for me

But it seems so right

I wish that you could also see

Am I being selfish?

for hoping that you'd end up with me

Because maybe you're not mine

maybe we're not meant to be

FAMILIAR STRANGER

I see you,

familiar stranger

my heart recognises

what my eyes refuse to see

It's been so long

since we were close

your touch but

a distant memory

The faintest brush past

my skin remembers

the way it felt

you lying next to me

We pass each other by

familiar strangers

no backward glance

not meant to be

YOU CANNOT ESCAPE ME

I am the sugar rolling over your tongue

oh so sweet

a taste you can't get rid of

I am the gentle caress of the wind

fingertips over bare skin

a shiver you can't shake off

I am the lips pressed to your ear

whispered melodies

a song you can't unhear

I am what you dream of

in the dark of night

 a sight you can't unsee

You may not love me, darling

you may not even like me

but you cannot escape me

MERCY

It's harder to fall

when there is something to lose

when there's no safety net to reach to

If it were up to me,

I'd run from all of this

this is not the path I'd choose

But I don't get a say, darling

we're at the mercy of the Universe

and for me, she's chosen you

PATIENCE

I know I must be patient
it is a virtue after all
but I don't want to wait
for you to also fall

I want our great love now
though time isn't on our side
but instead, I wait alone
for you to realise

I can be patient
and do what needs to be
I'll sacrifice what time I must
long as you end up with me

TAKE A CHANCE

Be gentle with me, darling
I'm still healing
a little rough around the edges
since he left me reeling

Be kind to me, darling
I'm still fragile
left picking glass shards out my heart
but I'll be worth your while

Be patient with me, darling
I'm finally on the mend
but it'll still be some time before
I learn to love again

I'll give you the world

If you can be gentle, patient, kind

I'm not defective, I'm not broken

I just need a little more time

EVERYWHERE BUT HERE

Glittering stars above

freckle the onyx sky

a faint reminder of

the glimmer in your eyes

Wind whips through my hair

it whispers in my ear

a familiar baritone

like you're really here

Crystal ocean waves

gently caress bare skin

it feels just like your touch

I'm ready to fall in

You are everywhere

in the sea, the stars, the sky

the only place you're not

is here, by my side

RIGHT PERSON, WRONG TIME

How can I wait

when I cannot breathe

and you're a

breath of fresh air

How can I wait

when you're all I see

after years in darkness

a blinding light

How can I wait

when I long to be touched

the anticipation of fingers

trailing over aching skin

And yet I must wait

the timing isn't right

there is much to be said

about right person, wrong time

DAYDREAM

For you,

I was just a foggy dream

fading, half-forgotten

by the time the sun

brightened the sky

and you opened your eyes

For me,

you were every

vivid daydream

hours spent escaping reality

caught up in the

idea of you and I

FINALLY RIGHT

You can push me away
you can ignore me
you can make every excuse
as to why we can't be

You can cast me aside
and be with someone new
pretend you hate me
but I know you felt it too

You don't have to hide from me
I'll give you your time
and if you're scared, darling,
I get it, so am I

It's okay to be unsure

it's been a long, ugly fight

but don't hold yourself back

we might finally have it right

WHISKY & WINE

I just want to go back

to that night

we got drunk on whisky & wine

and held each other tight

I laid bare my soul

& you didn't leave

it was how I knew

you were meant for me

So let's go get

drunk on

whisky & wine

I am yours, darling

if you are mine

MEMORY

People give me lectures that

I never remember

and I study for tests

but forget everything after

I find myself often

forgetting to hang out the washing

I can always recall

the lyrics to a good song

and I can recite

a poem I read years ago

and I'll always know your phone number

even though I haven't called in a while

I will never forget

the curve of your smile

or the sound of your laugh

or the heat from your touch

or the way that I felt

or what you meant to me

And I guess it's because

I only want to remember

what made me happy

CRAVE

I crave the deepest parts of you

show me your blackened soul

let me search every inch

and I'll ask for more, more, more

Surrender yourself to me

lay it all on the floor

confess every wicked deed

tell me every dark thought

I promise I won't shy

I just want to know you whole

I'll trace a claiming finger round

the jagged edges of your soul

I'll plant kisses along your scars

that zigzag across your heart

don't worry about them, darling,

they make you who you are

Give me everything

don't hold back, I want it all

the good parts of you are great

but it's the dark that makes me fall

LEAP OF FAITH

Are we destined for more?

how long will we dance
around each other
waiting for the other
to make the first move

Shall I jump first, darling
or shall we jump together?

PART IV – MINE

SEALED WITH AN X

What are we

to one another

where do we stand

I'm left to wonder

Talk all night

dream all day

of you and us and

things you say

 Await your replies

with bated breath

and you seal our fate

with an x

DANGEROUS

I've never looked at someone

the way I look at you

and that's how I know

this is dangerous

HEAT

Reach through the dark

fingers brush against

naked skin

gaze lingering

body built for sin

Hungry lips pressed

flush against my neck

breath hitched

smooth skin tingling

hope this never ends

Devilish look in your eye

starts a fire inside

share that heat

kisses burning

give yourself to me

THREAD OF FATE

A part of me loved you

before I ever knew you

a thread of fate

tangled 'round our two souls

The thread may tighten

as we pull away

from one another

but it will never let go

I will always

come back to you

COMING HOME

Cold feet on warm thighs

skin pressed to skin

the light in your eyes

drags me further in

Unravelled and undressed

fingers intertwined

head laid upon your chest

it whispers that you're mine

With you, I'm seeing stars

together, we're never alone

being in your arms

feels like coming home

THIS IS HOW IT FEELS

This is how it feels

to finally have you….

Right.

HALF OF MY SOUL

A soft hand snaking up my thigh

the curve of your lips pulled into a smile

an arched back, a breathy sigh

bask in each other's light a while

Fingers woven in the sheets

eyes squeezed closed, mouth slack

restless breaths between heartbeats

the trail of fingers down your back

I never want to leave you

when morning comes around

you've found home within me, too

missing half of my soul found

YOU ARE WHITE NOISE

You are rain

on an old tin roof

thundering white noise

that drowns out thoughts

 swirling around my

cluttered brain

My head is only quiet

when I look at you

a million thoughts

silenced by only one;

Mine

ETERNITY OF CONTENTMENT

Contentment is looking out the car window

watching the sun trace down the sky

driving past the vast blue ocean

your warm hand resting on my thigh

Contentment is a morning spent in bed

sheets tangled 'round bare legs

listening to the melody of your heartbeat

with your lips pressed to my forehead

Contentment is comfortable silence

the sound of games played while I read

sweet glances from each end of the couch

quiet company is all we need

Contentment is a trailing touch
fingertips brushing over smooth skin
with closed eyes and deep breaths
each stroke building calm within

Contentment is an eternity of you
living life together, our own way
getting myself lost in your laugh
day after day after day after day

PART V – METAMORPHOSIS

WHO AM I?

I hid parts of myself away

for so long

I forgot they existed

I made myself into what the world wanted

soft, but not weak

feminine, but not high maintenance

sensual, but not slutty

The hidden parts withered

discarded and neglected

until they became the distant fragments

of a girl that was

The mirror reflected back at me

something unrecognisable

something both terrible

and brimming with potential

A girl caught between who she really is

and who she was told to be

THE QUESTION

There comes a time where you must decide

if being accepted by society

is worth the price of losing who you are

Ask the question:

who would you be

in a world

where it was okay

to love yourself?

DOTTED LINE

If my lips are roses,

and my skin is snow,

tell me why

I am so alone?

If my hair is silk,

and my eyes are meadows,

tell me why

I have no place to go?

If my laugh is a melody,

and my mind is a diamond,

tell me why

I sit bathed in silence?

Because my lips are carnations,

my skin is chocolate chip,

my hair is tangled web,

my eyes are drains,

my laughter is the crack of a whip,

and my mind is a hurricane.

Is this why no one can love me?

because I am a dotted line

absent of a name?

CAN'T GO BACK

I keep looking to my past
trying to get back to who
 I was before you hurt me

But I can't go back
there's a reason that version
lies in the past, permanently

I have to push forward
no matter how unsure
and carve out a new identity

I suppose I am scared
that after all this time
you wouldn't recognise me

FLAWLESS

I fought parts of myself

suppressed the undesirable

caged it away

deep within myself

I repainted the surface

a pretty, perfect picture

no room for error, emotion

only desire and a smile

I became what they wanted

what was expected

half of a whole trapped beneath

a flawless mirror surface

Those parts of me broke through

the picture now restored

I settled into my new form and thought

is it true beauty if it isn't flawed?

YOU ARE WHAT YOU READ; YOU ARE WHO YOU MEET

I am an entanglement of tales

whispered and kept

snippets of all the people

I've ever met

I am the lines of every book

read to escape

the same damn words

filling in a different shape

I am a patchwork of

love songs stitched together

with all the poems

that speak about forever

I am not original

I'm made of scraps picked off the floor

a collection of feelings felt

a million times before

SOUL

Tread lightly through

the underbrush of my soul

it's dark out here

though some flowers still grow

Pay no mind

to the lingering darkness

it's better to wonder

than to know

Take a seat

amongst delicate blooms

bask in the moonlight's

faint radiating glow

Soak in the silence

if you dare listen

102

the wind will whisper

what you need know

Tread with care when

drifting through my soul

it's dark out here

and yet flowers still grow

JUXTAPOSITION

I am a wild winter storm

unpredictable and raging

yet calm as the rippling sea

I am a crackling fire

warm and inviting

yet hard and definite as steel

I am a bitter pill to swallow

caught in your throat

yet slick and sweet like honey

I am living juxtaposition

all hard angles butting

against soft subtlety

Come now, darling,

wouldn't it be fun

to get to know me?

HARDLY DEFINED

The picture you've built

of me in your mind

is only half the image

I am not something

that can be defined;

an elusive visage

There's more to me

than you might think –

you should already know this

Stay with me

and you might see

what lies beneath the surface

OPEN BOOK

Brutally honest or

just brutal?

You want an opinion?

I have several

I'm an open book

but be careful

Don't ask questions

you don't want answers to

DUALITY OF WOMAN

"You can't be both

beautiful and smart"

they say as they

try to suppress me

"You'd be so much prettier

if you wore less makeup"

they say as they

try to undress me

As if I give a fuck

about what they say

as if their respect

I would care to lose

Keep your thoughts

to yourself

I can be what I want

why should I have to choose

I'll be whatever

the hell pleases me

I won't bend to your will

I refuse

THIS ISN'T A POEM, IT'S A PROMISE

I'm done waiting

waiting to be wanted

instead, I'll want myself

I'll discover all the

 little things about me

that you only find out

when you're alone

and I'm going to love it

because it'll be

the closest anyone

has ever gotten to

knowing the real me

I can't wait to see

what she's like

ALONE BUT NOT LONELY

Being alone doesn't scare me

I like my own company

There's no one who gets it

quite like me

I may be alone

but I'm far from lonely

STRANGER // FRIEND

Take the time to know yourself
really know yourself
who are you when you're alone
away from everything else

Examine every inch
detail every flaw
learn to love the differences
that make you who you are

Take the time to know yourself
piece together what's been broken
love every jagged bit
it's all you have in the end

Don't be a stranger to yourself
be a friend

METAMORPHOSIS

At sixteen,

I thought

the most power a woman can have

is through people wanting you

At twenty-four,

I have learnt

the best sort of power

comes from wanting yourself

POWER

Why did it take

twenty-four years

to feel at home

in my own skin

For way too long

 I couldn't see

that I am good enough

that I am worthy

I don't need approval

from anybody else

I get all that I need

from myself

I've rebuilt that home

stronger than ever

114

a woman to be feared

a force to be reckoned

Now I'm finally here

not giving that power up

not for adoration

not even for love

ABOUT THE AUTHOR

R J O'Donnell is an indie author from Western Australia. Her writing interests are young adult/new adult dystopian fiction, fantasy and poetry.

Outside of writing, R J is a physiotherapist, working in aged care. She spends most of her free time working on her latest project, reading, playing netball and binging Netflix.

INFIRMITY, her debut young adult novel, was published in July 2021. The sequel to *INFIRMITY* is set to be released early 2023. R J also has a young adult fantasy novel in the works, release date TBA.

STAY UPDATED

Stay updated on all the latest writing news
from R J O'DONNELL

TIKTOK: @rjodo

FACEBOOK: R J O'Donnell- Author
@RJODonnellAuthor

INSTAGRAM: @r.j.odonnell

Lightning Source UK Ltd.
Milton Keynes UK
UKHW041623170222
398778UK00010B/218